POWER
YESTERDAY • TODAY • TOMORROW

ENERGY FROM ATOMS

NUCLEAR POWER

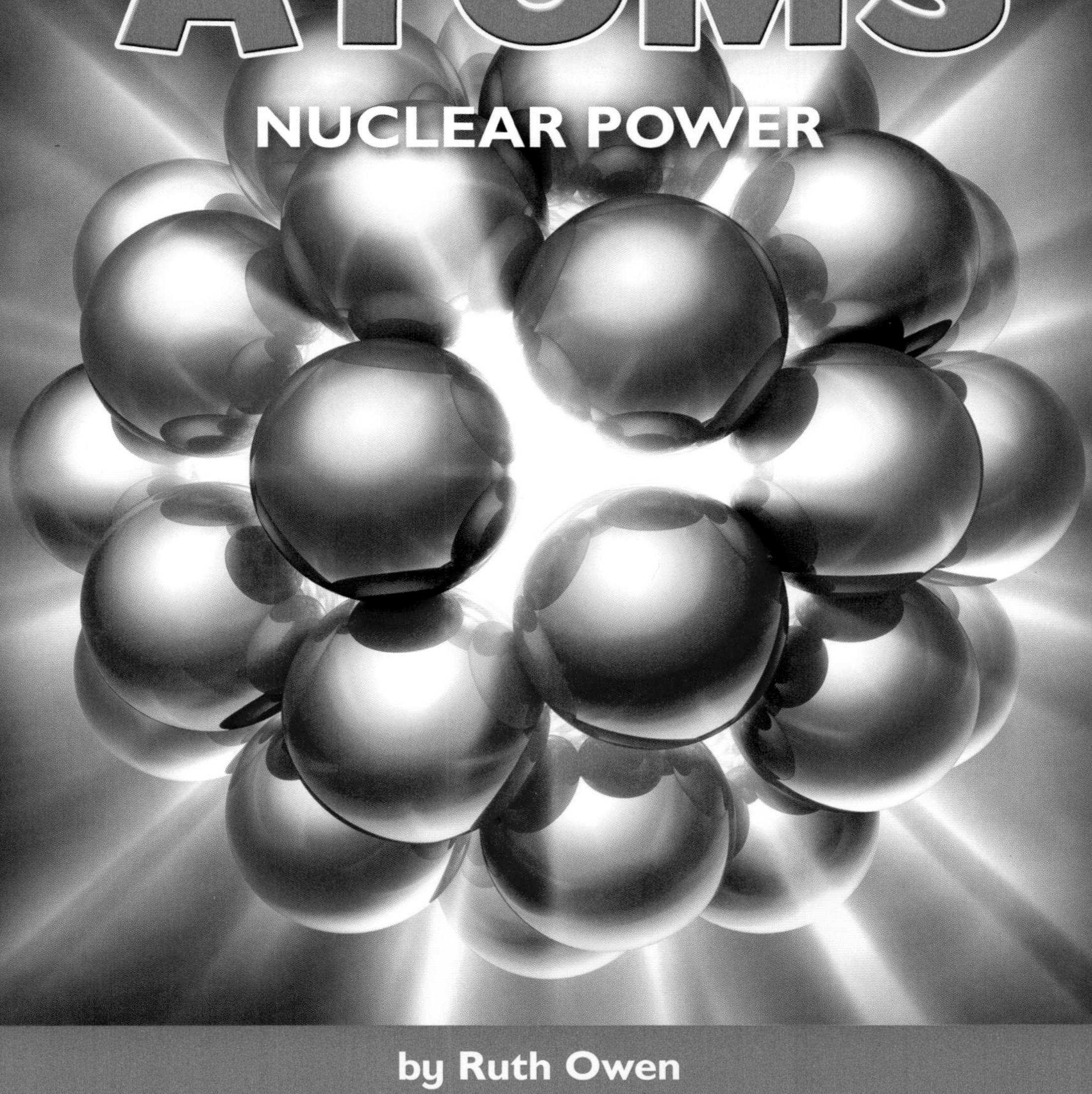

by Ruth Owen

PowerKiDS press.
New York

Published in 2013 by The Rosen Publishing Group, Inc.
29 East 21st Street, New York, NY 10010

Produced for Rosen by Ruby Tuesday Books Ltd
Editor for Ruby Tuesday Books Ltd: Mark J. Sachner
US Editor: Sara Antill
Designer: Emma Randall
Consultant: Jeanine Gelhaus, M.S.; K-12 Energy Education Program, University of Wisconsin-Stevens Point

Photo Credits:
Cover, 1, 2–3, 4–5, 7, 8–9, 18 (bottom), 23 (top), 26–27, 28–29 © Shutterstock; 8, 13, 14–15, 16–17 © Science Photo Library; 10–11, 21, 22, 25 (bottom) © Wikipedia Creative Commons; 12 (top), 18–19 © Alamy; 12 (bottom) © United States Nuclear Regulatory Committee; 20 © Melvin A. Miller of the Argonne National Laboratory; 23 (bottom) © Chernobyl Museum, Kiev; 24 © Kawamoto Takuo, Wikipedia Creative Commons; 25 (top) © Corbis.

Publisher Cataloging Data

Owen, Ruth, 1967–
Energy from atoms : nuclear power / by Ruth Owen.
p. cm. — (Power: yesterday, today, tomorrow)
Includes index.
Summary: This book describes how nuclear energy is generated, examines the pros and cons of using nuclear energy as a source of power, tells of the importance of finding sources of energy other than fossil fuels, and more.
Contents: Powering our world with nuclear energy — Electricity, fossil fuels, and climate change — Splitting atoms — Understanding radiation — Uranium—fuel for nuclear power — A nuclear reactor — More reactor facts — Nuclear waste — A brief history of nuclear energy — The Chernobyl nuclear disaster — The Fukushima nuclear disaster — Nuclear power—the arguments — A nuclear-powered future?
ISBN 978-1-4777-0272-7 (library binding) — ISBN 978-1-4777-0283-3 (pbk.) —
ISBN 978-1-4777-0284-0 (6-pack)≠
1. Nuclear energy—Juvenile literature 2. Nuclear power plants—Juvenile literature [1. Nuclear energy 2. Nuclear power plants 3. Power resources]
I. Title
2013
333.792/4—dc23

Manufactured in the United States of America

CPSIA Compliance Information: Batch #W13PK7: For Further Information contact Rosen Publishing, New York, New York at 1-800-237-9932

CONTENTS

Powering Our World with Nuclear Energy 4

Electricity, Fossil Fuels, and Climate Change 6

Splitting Atoms 8

Understanding Radiation 10

Uranium—Fuel for Nuclear Power 12

A Nuclear Reactor 14

More Reactor Facts 16

Nuclear Waste 18

A Brief History of Nuclear Energy 20

The Chernobyl Nuclear Disaster 22

The Fukushima Nuclear Disaster 24

Nuclear Power—The Arguments 26

A Nuclear-Powered Future? 28

Glossary 30

Websites 31

Read More, Index 32

Powering Our World with Nuclear Energy

Is there an industry that can reliably generate electricity into the future and help combat **climate change**? Does that same industry have the potential to cause catastrophic disasters that create waste materials, which will remain highly dangerous long after everyone alive today is gone?

In nuclear power stations, electricity is produced using the huge quantities of energy that are released when **atoms** are split apart. This method of producing power is probably the world's most controversial way of generating electricity.

Politicians, scientists, people within the nuclear industry, environmental activists, and ordinary members of the public all have opinions on whether the world should or should not use nuclear energy to produce power.

One thing is for certain—our modern world needs electricity. In the United States today, around 70 percent of electricity is

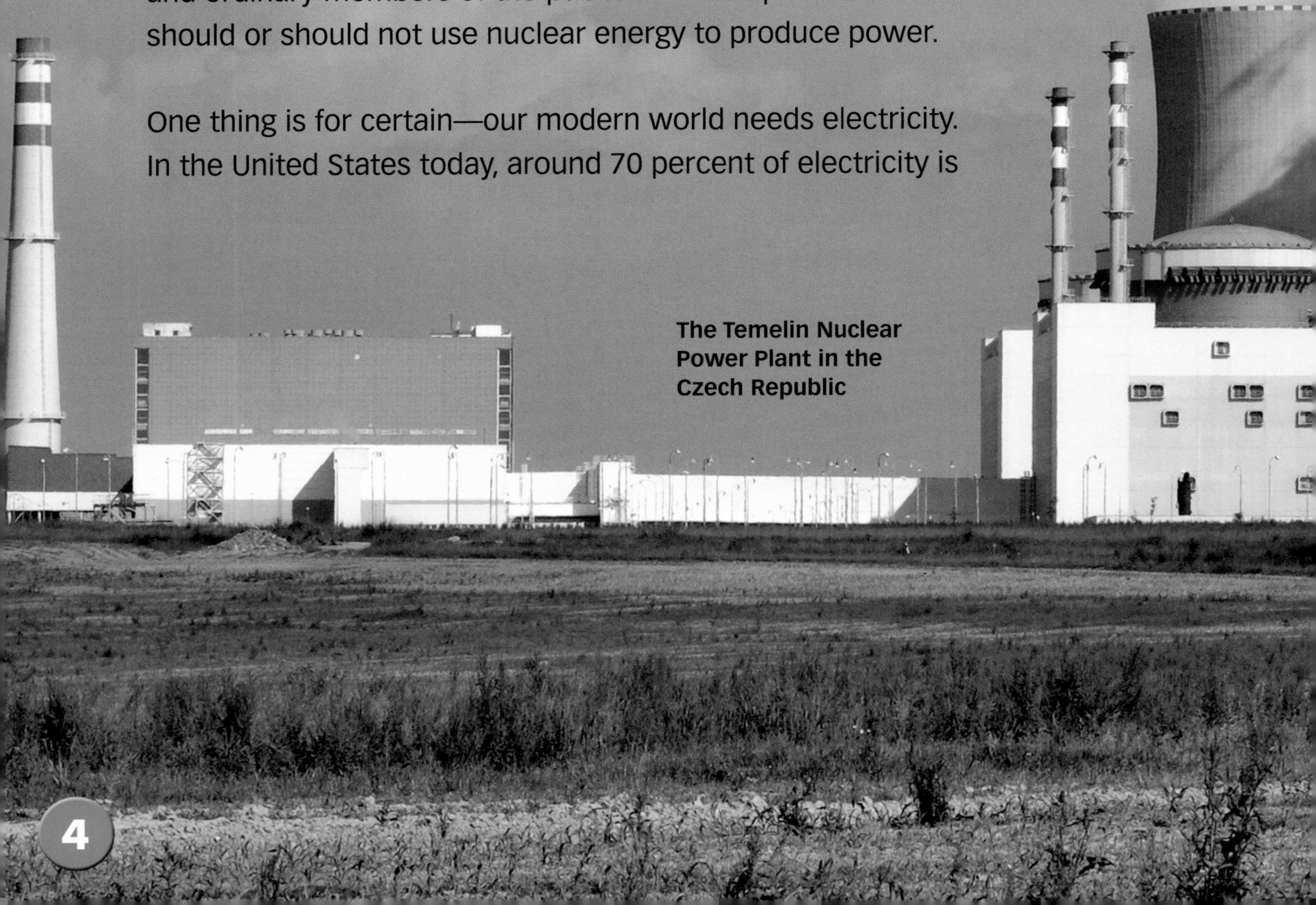

The Temelin Nuclear Power Plant in the Czech Republic

generated using coal and **natural gas**. This situation cannot continue, however, because these fuels are running out fast, and their use is leading to climate change.

Many people believe that nuclear power is the answer to powering our world into the future. Others believe that nuclear power can only become a recipe for disaster!

Unlike power stations that burn coal and gas and release pollution into the air, the chimneys at this nuclear power station are only releasing steam as part of the electricity-generation process.

FAST FACT

The United States currently uses nuclear energy to generate about 20 percent of its electricity. South Korea and many European countries, including Belgium, the Czech Republic, Sweden, and Ukraine, obtain over 30 percent of their power from nuclear energy. In France, 75 percent of the nation's electricity comes from nuclear power stations.

Electricity, Fossil Fuels, and Climate Change

Much of the electricity used worldwide today is generated by burning coal and natural gas.

At coal-fired or gas-fired power stations, these fuels are burned inside huge boilers to heat water to such a high temperature that it becomes steam. Then the steam is used to spin giant **turbines**, which power **generators** that produce electricity.

There are big problems, however, with producing electricity using coal and natural gas.

Known as **fossil fuels**, these fuels formed from the remains of ancient plants and animals. Over millions of years, heat and pressure underground turned the remains into coal, oil, and natural gas. Now the Earth's stocks of fossil fuels are running out, and we cannot make more.

Also, when we burn fossil fuels, gases such as carbon dioxide, methane, and nitrous oxide are released into the Earth's **atmosphere**. Known as **greenhouse gases**, these gases trap the Sun's heat on Earth, just as a greenhouse traps heat inside. This is causing a gradual increase in Earth's temperatures that most scientists agree is leading to climate change.

Like coal and natural gas, nuclear energy can be used as a fuel in power stations. The big difference, however, is that generating electricity with nuclear energy does not produce greenhouse gases.

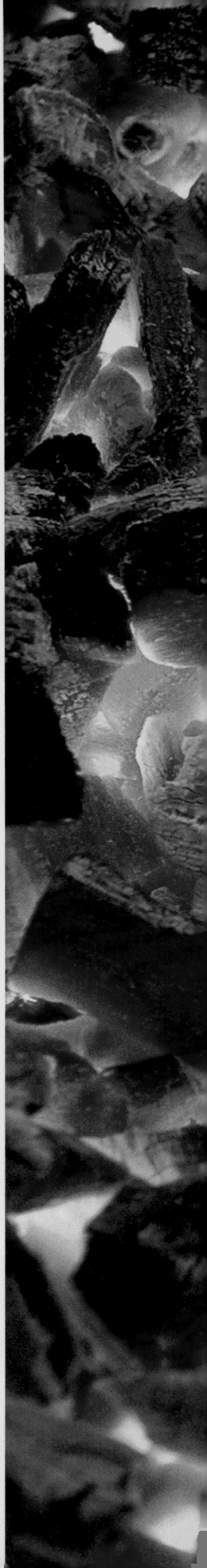

In some parts of the world, climate change will cause the weather to become so hot and dry that water supplies will dry up and people will not be able to grow crops.

New York City

FAST FACT

Warmer temperatures due to climate change will cause ocean levels to rise, because water expands when it is heated. Also, ice at the North and South poles will melt. This will lead to flooding in low-lying coastal places, including cities such as New York and London.

Coal, natural gas, and oil are nonrenewable resources because it's not possible to make more of them.

Splitting Atoms

Nuclear energy is the energy that is released when an atom is split. Atoms are tiny particles that can only be seen with specialized microscopes, such as the **electron microscope**. Every object in the universe is made up of atoms.

In a nuclear power station, the atoms that are split are **uranium** atoms. Uranium is a metal that is found in rocks all over the world and in seawater. The uranium atoms are split in a process called **nuclear fission**.

During nuclear fission, a particle called a **neutron** smashes into a uranium atom and splits it. A huge amount of energy, or heat, is released from the uranium atom along with **radiation** and two or three more neutrons. The neutrons that have been released from the uranium atom then smash into other uranium atoms and split them, releasing more energy, more radiation, and more neutrons. This process happens again and again, millions of times over, in a chain reaction.

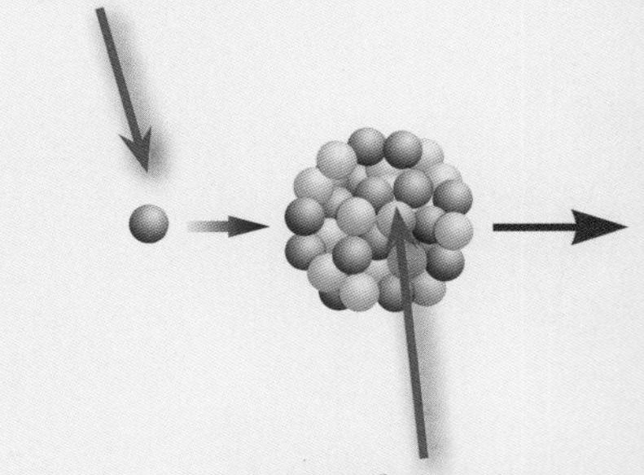

The heat that is released by nuclear fission is used in the power station to heat water to create steam, which spins the turbines that drive the electrical generators.

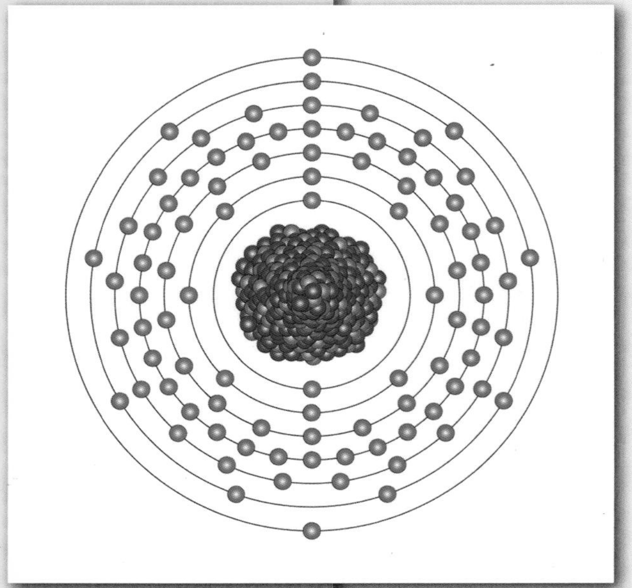

This is a diagram of a uranium atom. It has protons (red) and neutrons (blue) inside its nucleus. The electrons (green) are orbiting the nucleus.

A Nuclear Chain Reaction

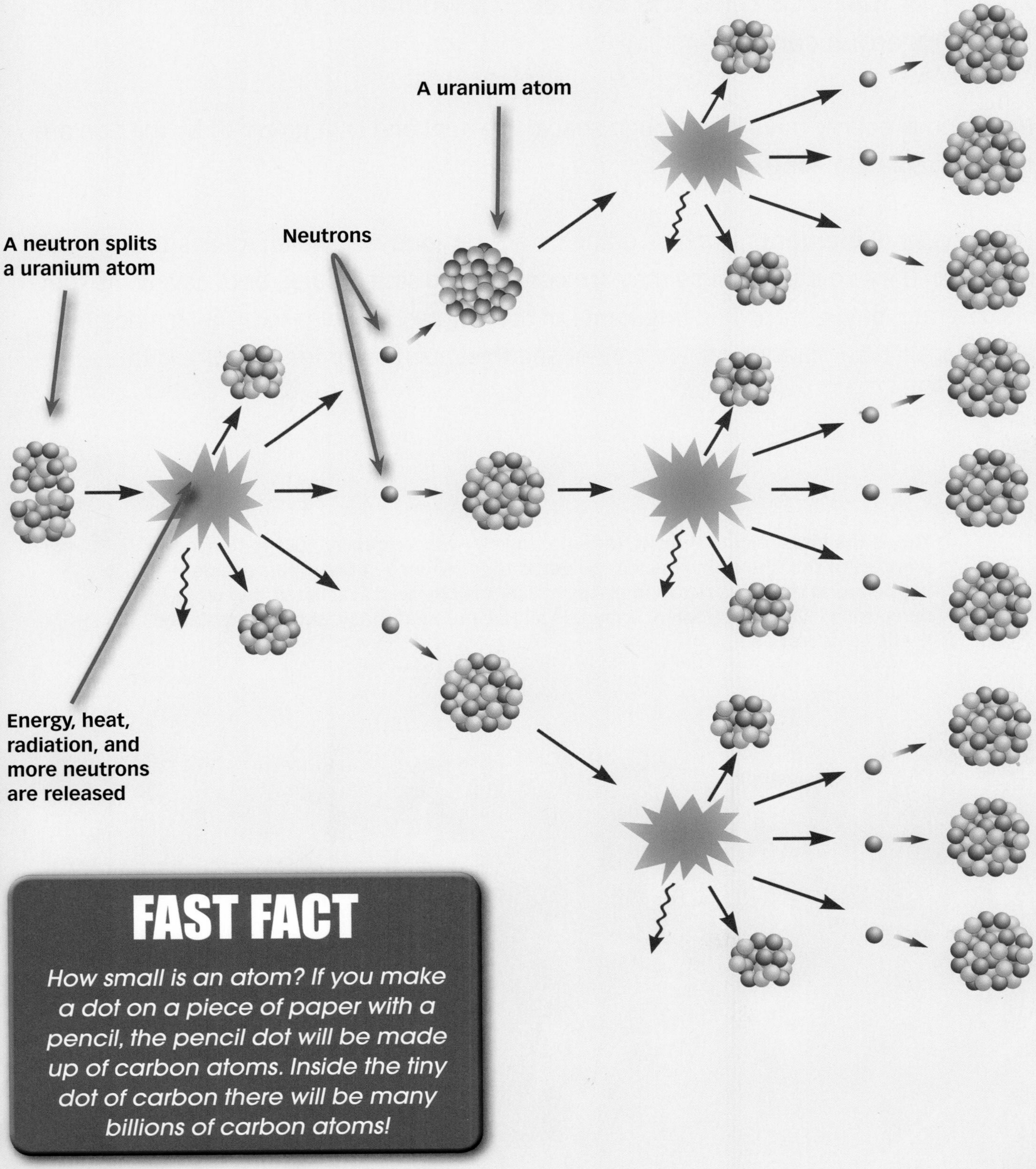
A uranium atom
A neutron splits
a uranium atom
Neutrons
Energy, heat,
radiation, and
more neutrons
are released

FAST FACT

How small is an atom? If you make a dot on a piece of paper with a pencil, the pencil dot will be made up of carbon atoms. Inside the tiny dot of carbon there will be many billions of carbon atoms!

Understanding Radiation

When nuclear energy is discussed, the word "radiation" will always come up. You may have heard that radiation can escape from a nuclear power station, or that it can give you **cancer**. But what exactly is radiation, and how dangerous can it be?

Radiation is energy traveling through space. The heat and light given off by the Sun are types of radiation, for example.

Some types of **elements**, such as uranium, are **radioactive**, which means they give off radiation. They do this because they are constantly disintegrating, or decaying. As they disintegrate, tiny, fast-moving fragments of their atoms are released. These pieces of atoms are a type of radiation. We cannot see this radiation or feel it, but it is there.

This is the ghost city of Pripyat, Ukraine. The city was originally built to house the workers of the Chernobyl nuclear power station. When a catastrophic accident happened at the power station in April 1986, the city was evacuated due to dangerous levels of radiation. Pripyat is still abandoned today, although radiation levels have dropped.

The uranium in rocks all over the world is constantly giving off very low levels of radiation that is not usually dangerous. When uranium atoms are split during nuclear fission, however, they give off much greater levels of radiation.

If people or animals come into contact with high levels of radiation from uranium, it can cause sickness, cancer, and even death. At a nuclear power station, the radiation is contained so that it cannot escape into the air and harm workers or people outside.

FAST FACT

Whether or not people have been harmed by exposure to radiation from nuclear power stations is one area of disagreement between different groups of scientists. While all scientists agree that high levels of radiation can cause damage to a human body, they do not always agree on how high those levels have to be or what damage might be caused.

The Chernobyl nuclear power station is shut down and is inside an exclusion zone where there are still high radiation levels.

Uranium—Fuel for Nuclear Power

Just like fossil fuels, uranium, the fuel that is used in nuclear power stations, is a nonrenewable fuel source and will one day run out.

One way that uranium is collected is by mining it from underground rock or from rock on the Earth's surface. The rock is crushed and a liquid, such as sulfuric acid, is used to dissolve the uranium so it separates from the rock.

The dissolved uranium is then removed from the liquid, dried, and stored in drums as a powder known as yellowcake. The yellowcake undergoes many processes until finally, it is compressed into fuel pellets, which are then loaded into long metal tubes known as fuel rods.

Fuel rods are the thickness of pencils, and can be up to 14 feet (4.3 m) long. They are made of metal to help contain the radioactive material inside. The fuel rods are grouped together in bundles called **fuel assemblies**. Each fuel assembly may contain over 200 fuel rods. The fuel assemblies are used in nuclear power stations to create heat.

A drum of yellowcake

This nuclear fuel pellet, smaller than a person's fingertip, contains as much energy as 1,780 pounds (807 kg) of coal.

FAST FACT

Elements may occur in different forms called isotopes. Uranium occurs in the Earth's crust in two different isotopes. About 99.3 percent of the uranium on Earth is uranium 238. The other 0.7 percent is uranium 235. Even though uranium 235 is more rare, nuclear power stations use it as fuel because its atoms split apart more easily than uranium 238.

This fuel assembly is being moved by a machine to limit the exposure of workers at the nuclear power station to the radioactive fuel pellets inside the fuel rods.

A Nuclear Reactor

At a coal-fired power station, coal is burned in a boiler to heat water. At a nuclear power station, the water is heated by nuclear fission inside a **nuclear reactor**.

At the center of a nuclear reactor is the **core**. Inside the core, hundreds of fuel assemblies are placed in water. Nuclear fission takes place inside the fuel assemblies, and the extreme heat that is generated boils the water so that it turns to steam.

The steam is used to turn the power station's huge turbines, which make the generators spin and produce electricity. The steam is then cooled down so it condenses back into water and can be used again.

The electricity generated at the power station is carried through power lines to homes, businesses, and any other place where it is needed.

Back inside the reactor, the nuclear fission process is controlled by rods. These control rods absorb neutrons and can be inserted into the reactor or withdrawn to control the rate at which fission happens. The control rods are also used to shut down the reactor in an emergency situation.

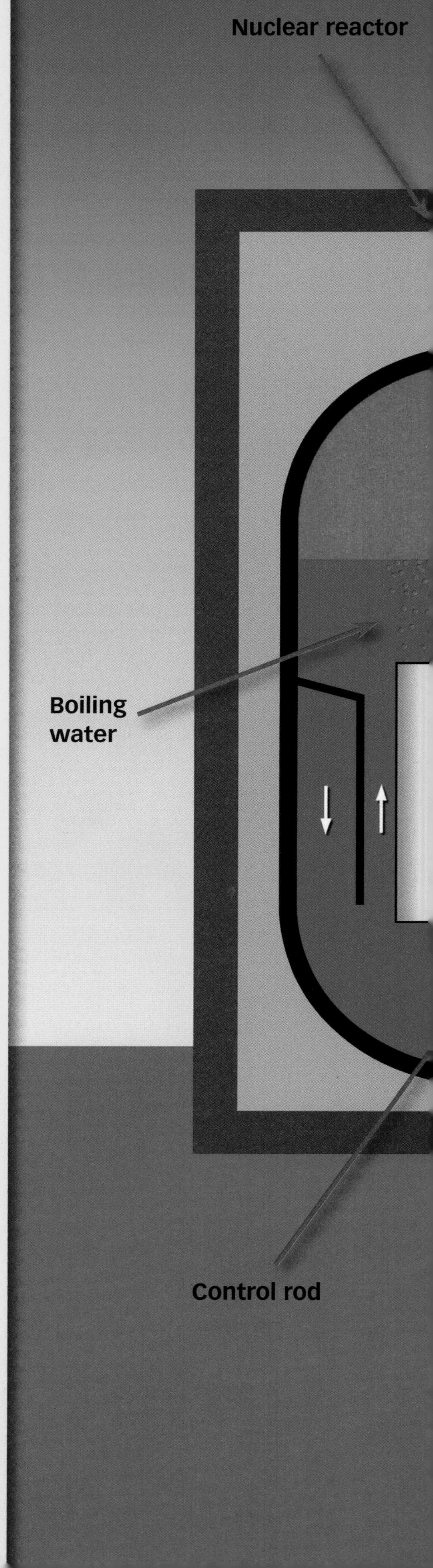

This diagram shows how nuclear power is used to generate electricity at a nuclear power station.

FAST FACT

Uranium has a much higher heat value than coal. A one million ***kilowatt*** *coal-fired power station burns about 3.5 million tons (3.2 million t) of coal each year. A one million kilowatt nuclear power station only uses 26.5 tons (24 t) of uranium, which will be extracted from 22,000 tons (20,000 t) of rock.*

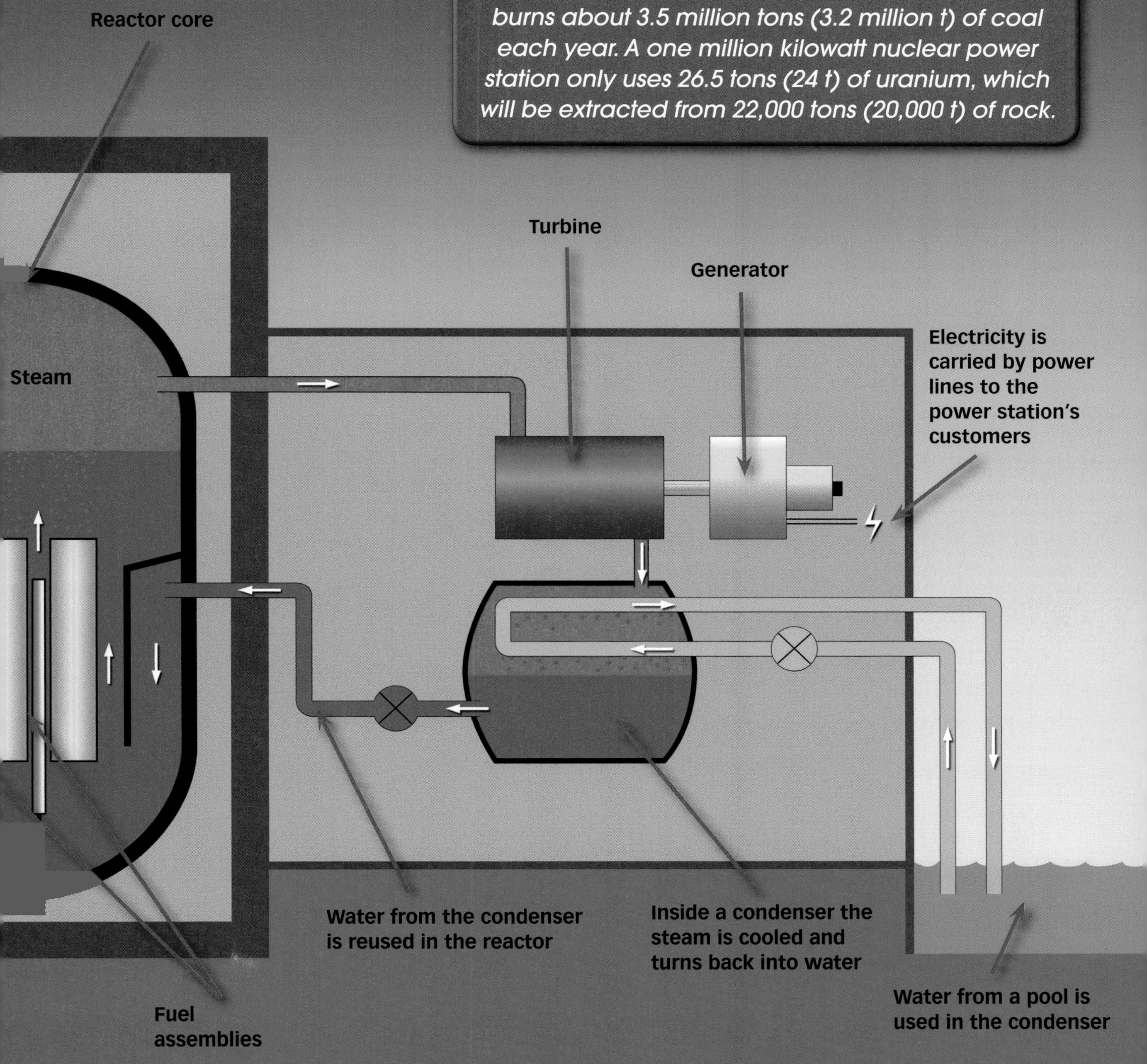
Reactor core
Turbine
Generator
Steam
Electricity is carried by power lines to the power station's customers
Water from the condenser is reused in the reactor
Inside a condenser the steam is cooled and turns back into water
Water from a pool is used in the condenser
Fuel assemblies

More Reactor Facts

In the United States, two types of nuclear reactors are used—boiling-water reactors and pressurized-water reactors.

In a boiling-water reactor, water in the reactor's core is boiled and turns directly to steam. This steam is then used to drive the turbines, as shown in the diagram on pages 14–15.

In a pressurized-water reactor, the water in the core is kept under pressure so that it remains a liquid and doesn't turn to steam. The hot, radioactive water then passes through a steam generator. This piece of equipment is a giant cylinder that contains thousands of tubes and is filled with clean, nonradioactive water. The hot, radioactive water from the reactor flows through the cylinder's tubes, and its heat is then used to turn the nonradioactive water in the cylinder into steam, which powers the turbines.

The radioactive water then passes back into the reactor core to be reheated and used again. The clean, nonradioactive water in the steam generator cylinder usually comes from a source alongside the power station, such as a river, lake, or ocean.

New fuel assemblies, to replace used ones, are lowered into the core of a pressurized-water nuclear reactor.

FAST FACT

To prevent harmful uranium radiation from escaping from a nuclear power station, fuel rods are encased in metal. The nuclear reactor's core is enclosed in a special covering called a pressure vessel, and the whole reactor is inside a containment structure that prevents the release of radiation.

Nuclear Waste

A fuel assembly stays in a nuclear reactor for about four and a half years. Then, the highly radioactive used fuel must be removed and stored until its levels of radiation die down.

To protect a power station's workers, every step of the removal process is done underwater so the water contains the radiation that is being given off. From the reactor, the used fuel assembly is transferred to a large pool, where it must remain underwater for many years. The pool's water cools the fuel assembly and contains its radiation. At some power stations, used fuel assemblies are stored in special steel or concrete containers, which are cooled down using air.

Even after an initial storage period, the waste must still be contained. Some countries are developing plans to bury nuclear waste in rock at least 1,600 feet (500 m) underground at special burial sites. The waste must then remain buried for thousands of years! After this time, the waste's level of radioactivity will be safe, and similar to the amount given off by uranium when it is naturally found in rock.

This symbol (in magenta or black on a yellow background) is used worldwide to show that materials are radioactive, or to warn people that they may be exposed to radiation.

Used fuel assemblies stored in a pool beneath 30 feet (9 m) of water at the Crystal River Nuclear Plant, in Florida

FAST FACT

Depending on the type of power plant, some used nuclear fuel may go through a process that recycles the waste so that it can be used again as fuel in a nuclear power station. About 97 percent of the waste can be reused as fuel, leaving just 3 percent as highly radioactive waste that needs to be contained.

A Brief History of Nuclear Energy

By the late 1700s, when uranium was discovered, scientists had for centuries been forming ideas about the atom as a basic unit of matter.

This is a drawing of Chicago Pile 1, the world's first nuclear reactor. It was built by a team that included physicists Enrico Fermi and Leo Szilard, discoverer of the chain reaction. Chicago Pile 1 was built under an abandoned sports stadium at the University of Chicago.

It was only in the 1930s and early 1940s, however, that scientists discovered that smashing an atom's nucleus with neutrons would create nuclear fission and the release of energy. In 1942, during World War II, scientists meeting in Chicago developed the world's first nuclear reactor, and with it, the world's first chain reaction.

Following this achievement, the United States began developing the technology to unleash the power of the atom in the form of a bomb. In August 1945, the United States exploded two atomic bombs over Japan, one over the city of Hiroshima, and the other over Nagasaki. These bombings put an end to World War II. They also resulted in unimaginable destruction and the deaths of an estimated 200,000 Japanese people.

After the war, scientists began finding ways to use the atom to supply energy for peaceful purposes. In 1957, the first commercial nuclear-powered electrical plant started up in Shippingport, Pennsylvania.

FAST FACT

In 1951, usable electricity was produced for the first time in a test at an experimental reactor in Arco, Idaho. The test resulted in the lighting of four electric light bulbs. By 1955, the entire town had become the first community in the world to be lit by electricity generated by nuclear power!

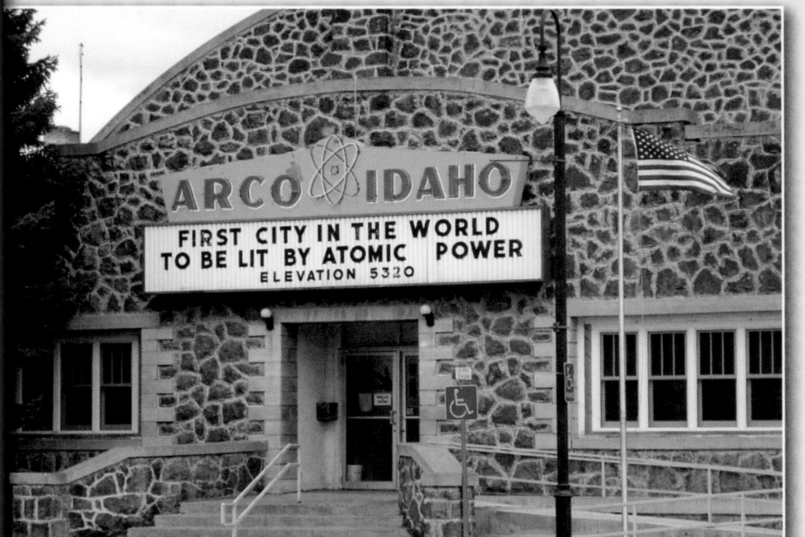

A building in Arco, Idaho, proudly proclaims the city's nuclear-powered history.

The Chernobyl Nuclear Disaster

On Saturday, April 26, 1986, a safety test was carried out on reactor number 4 at the Chernobyl nuclear power station in Ukraine. During the test, a crew of inexperienced workers lost control of the reactor. Temperatures rose, the emergency shutdown failed, and the reactor exploded!

A photograph of reactor number 4 taken from a helicopter on May 3, 1986

A shower of lethal radioactive material was blasted into the air. Over the days that followed, this radiation was blown by the wind into neighboring Belarus and Russia.

In 1986, Ukraine was part of the Soviet Union. The secretive Soviet government did not want the world to know what had happened and didn't ask for help. Firefighters and other workers who were not trained to deal with a nuclear disaster took 10 days to control the radioactive emissions coming from the reactor.

Hundreds of thousands of people were evacuated from their homes because radiation levels were too high in their villages, towns, and cities. Today, it is still too dangerous to live in the exclusion zone, an area within 20 miles (30 km) of the power station.

The Chernobyl nuclear disaster terrified the world. It showed what can go wrong at a nuclear power station if it is not operated safely and expertly.

Scenes from the abandoned city of Pripyat inside the Chernobyl exclusion zone

FAST FACT

Even today, experts cannot agree on what the full health implications are for the people touched by the Chernobyl radiation cloud. One thing that all experts agree on is that tens of thousands of people affected by the disaster have contracted or will contract thyroid cancer during their lives because of their exposure to radiation.

Photographed in 1996, these children were born in 1987 and 1988 to families in Pripyat (the nearest city to the disaster) and to liquidators, the people who worked at the power station in the aftermath of the disaster. Many of the children now have health problems.

The Fukushima Nuclear Disaster

The reactor number 1 building at the Fukushima Daiichi nuclear power station in 1999

Nuclear reactors must be designed and built to withstand fires, floods, tornadoes, hurricanes, earthquakes, and tsunamis. Things can still go terribly wrong, however.

On March 11, 2011, a massive earthquake happened off the east coast of Japan. All power from the country's main **electrical power grid** was lost. Nuclear power stations in operation at the time shut down their reactors as a safety measure. They also used backup electrical generators to run systems that would cool down the reactors. Everything worked exactly as it should.

Then, an hour after the earthquake, a 49-foot-(15 m) high tsunami, or tidal wave, hit the coast. The Fukushima Daiichi nuclear power station was flooded and lost all backup generator power. The power station's cooling systems could no longer operate, and water around the fuel assemblies in the reactor cores began to boil away. Rising temperatures caused fires and explosions, sending radioactive material into the air. Within three days, news of a reactor meltdown spread around the world.

FAST FACT

One way to ensure that a nuclear disaster like Fukushima never happens again is to have a backup power system in a different location than the power station itself. Then if a natural disaster damages the power station, the backup power might not be affected.

The remains of the reactor number 1 building photographed by an unmanned drone aircraft on April 12, 2011

Since the Fukushima Daiichi disaster, many people in Japan no longer want nuclear power stations. Here, people take part in an antinuclear rally in Tokyo, Japan, in September 2011.

Nuclear Power—The Arguments

Making electricity with nuclear energy does not create greenhouse gases, but what other benefits are there to using nuclear power, and what are the downsides?

Nuclear Power Pros

- *In a section of the Earth's crust that covers 1 square mile (2.5 sq. km) and is 1 foot (0.3 m) deep, there will be about 1 ton (0.9 t) of uranium. This amount of uranium can produce the same amount of electricity as 16,000 tons (14,500 t) of coal!*
- *The safe running of nuclear reactors is a high priority in their design. Today, designs have improved from those used at the Chernobyl power station. Older power stations have been modified to make them safer.*
- *Many countries have to import fuel, such as coal, to make electricity. The smaller quantities of uranium that can be used to make electricity in a nuclear power station are easier and more economical to store.*
- *Scientists have estimated that there is enough uranium in the Earth's crust to fuel the world's nuclear power stations for about 100 years. If new, more efficient methods of extracting power from uranium are used, however, stocks could last for up to 2,500 years!*
- *A joint program between Russia and the United States is taking uranium from unwanted nuclear weapons, from the days of the Soviet Union, and recycling it to be used in nuclear power stations in the United States.*

Nuclear Power Cons

Hundreds of studies have been carried out to investigate the link between nuclear power stations and cancer. Some studies show that people living near nuclear power stations are in no more danger of contracting cancer than people living elsewhere. Other studies disagree with these results. One thing for certain is that exposure to high levels of radiation will cause cancer.

A nuclear power station

To build a one million kilowatt wind farm, up to 180,000 acres (73,000 ha) of land would be needed. A nuclear power station producing the same amount of electricity will only require around 400 acres (162 ha) of land. However, if the nuclear power station stops production and is decommissioned, the land may be too dangerous to ever reuse.

Nuclear power reactors are very expensive to build. It also takes a very long time to build a nuclear power station.

Waste from nuclear power stations must be stored for thousands of years to prevent harmful radiation from being released. This type of storage is very expensive.

The nuclear power industry takes safety very seriously. However, accidents have happened. The potential for disaster is huge when dealing with nuclear energy and radiation.

A Nuclear-Powered Future?

Today, nuclear energy is used to produce about 14 percent of the world's electricity. It could produce much more, though.

A nuclear power station and solar panels are shown here. Do you feel that nuclear energy and "green" technologies, such as solar panels and wind turbines, should be combined to power our future?

We need electricity, and we need it to be generated without the creation of greenhouse gases. Nuclear power stations can produce electricity cleanly, efficiently, day and night, 365 days a year. Many people believe that used alongside environmentally-friendly forms of energy such as wind power and solar power, nuclear energy could be the answer to reducing the world's reliance on fossil fuels.

Other people are concerned about the potential danger of a nuclear disaster spreading radiation for hundreds of miles (km) around a nuclear power station. They feel that however small the danger, it is too high a price to pay for electricity.

Today, there are over 430 nuclear power stations in the world, with many more under construction. Some people want to build more. Others want the drive for more nuclear power to stop. The arguments will continue on both sides.

Will the future be nuclear powered? It's your future. What do you want?

FAST FACT

The Chernobyl and Fukushima nuclear disasters show us how dangerous nuclear power can be if something goes wrong. On the other hand, since the 1950s, the world's nuclear power stations have accumulated around 14,500 years of safe electricity production.

What would your response to more nuclear power be?

Glossary

atmosphere (AT-muh-sfeer)
The layer of gases surrounding a planet, moon, or star.

atom (A-tem)
The smallest particle of something, consisting of electrons, protons, and neutrons.

cancer (KAN-ser)
Any one of a number of diseases in which cells in a body multiply without control in an abnormal way and spread through the body, causing harm.

climate change (KLY-mut CHAYNJ)
The gradual change in temperatures on Earth. For example, the current warming of temperatures caused by a buildup of greenhouse gases in the atmosphere.

core (KOR)
The part of a nuclear reactor that contains the fuel assemblies. Nuclear fission takes place in a nuclear reactor's core.

electrical power grid
(ih-LEK-trih-kul POW-er GRID)
A system of power lines that connects homes and other buildings to electrical power stations.

electron microscope
(ih-LEK-tron MY-kruh-skohp)
A very powerful microscope that uses a beam of electrons to illuminate an item and produce a magnified image.

element (EH-luh-ment)
A chemical substance that consists of only one type of atom and cannot be broken down into a simpler substance by a chemical reaction.

fossil fuels (FO-sul FYOOLZ)
Fuels that formed over millions of years from the remains of plants and animals.

fuel assembly (FYOO-el uh-SEM-blee)
A bundle of metal fuel rods filled with pellets of uranium that are used as fuel in a nuclear reactor.

generator (JEH-neh-ray-tur)
A machine that turns mechanical energy, for example the spinning of a turbine, into electrical energy.

greenhouse gases
(GREEN-hows GAS-ez)
Gases such as carbon dioxide, methane, and nitrous oxide that occur naturally and are also released into Earth's atmosphere when fossil fuels are burned.

kilowatt (KIH-luh-waht)
A measure of electricity equal to 1,000 watts. A watt is a small unit of power. A kilowatt is enough electricity to power ten 100-watt light bulbs.

natural gas (NA-chuh-rul GAS)
A fossil fuel that formed underground over millions of years. It is piped to homes and businesses to be used as a source of energy.

neutron (NOO-tron)
A particle in the nucleus (the center part) of an atom that has no electrical charge.

nuclear fission (NOO-klee-ur FIH-shun)
The process in which atoms are split apart by neutrons again and again in a chain reaction.

nuclear reactor
(NOO-klee-ur ree-AK-tur)
The part of a nuclear power station that houses the core where nuclear fission takes place.

radiation (ray-dee-AY-shun)
Energy that is radiated in waves (light from the Sun) or in particles (radiation from uranium).

radioactive (ray-dee-oh-AK-tiv)
Giving off radiation.

turbine (TER-byn)
A machine with a wheel or rotor that turns and generates power. A turbine can be driven by gas, water, or steam.

uranium (yoo-RAY-nee-um)
A heavy, radioactive metal element found in rocks and seawater.

WEBSITES

Due to the changing nature of Internet links, PowerKids Press has developed an online list of websites related to the subject of this book. This site is updated regularly. Please use this link to access the list:

www.powerkidslinks.com/pytt/nucl/

Read More

Jakubiak, David J. *What Can We Do About Nuclear Waste?*. Protecting Our Planet. New York: PowerKids Press, 2012.

Reynoldson, Fiona. *Understanding Nuclear Power*. The World of Energy. New York: Gareth Stevens, 2011.

Spilsbury, Richard, and Louise Spilsbury. *Nuclear Power*. Let's Discuss Energy Resources. New York: PowerKids Press, 2012.

Index

A
Arco, Idaho, 21
atomic bombs, 21
atoms, 4, 8–11, 13, 20–21
atmosphere, 6

B
Belarus, 22
boiling-water reactors, 16

C
cancer, 10–11, 23, 27
carbon dioxide, 6
chain reactions, 8–9, 20–21
Chernobyl nuclear power station, 10–11, 22–23, 26, 29
Chicago Pile 1, 20
climate change, 4–7
coal, 5–7, 12, 14–15, 26
condensers, 15
control rods, 14–15
cores (of nuclear reactors), 14–17, 24
Czech Republic, 4–5

E
earthquakes, 24
electricity, 4–6, 14–15, 21, 26–29
electrons, 8

F
Fermi, Enrico, 20
fossil fuels, 6–7, 12, 28
France, 5
fuel assemblies, 12–19, 24
fuel pellets, 12–13
fuel rods, 12–13, 17
Fukushima Daiichi nuclear power station, 24–25, 29

G
generators, 6, 8, 14–15, 24
greenhouse gases, 6, 26, 28

H
heat, 6, 8–10, 12, 14, 16
Hiroshima, Japan, 21

I
isotopes, 13

M
methane, 6

N
Nagasaki, Japan, 21
natural gas, 5–7
neutrons, 8–9, 14, 21
nitrous oxide, 6
nuclear disasters, 4, 10–11, 22–25, 27–29
nuclear fission, 8–9, 11, 14–15, 21
nuclear reactors, 14–18, 20–22, 24–27
nuclear waste, 4, 18–19, 27
nuclear weapons, 26

O
oil, 6–7

P
pressure vessels, 17
pressurized-water reactors, 16–17
Pripyat, Ukraine, 10–11, 23
protons, 8

R
radiation, 8–11, 17–19, 22–24, 27–28
radioactivity, 10–13, 16, 18–19, 22, 24
Russia, 22, 26

S
seawater, 8
South Korea, 5
splitting atoms, 4, 8–9, 11, 13
steam, 5–6, 8, 14–16
steam generators, 16
sulfuric acid, 12
Sun, 6, 10
Szilard, Leo, 20

T
tsunamis, 24
turbines, 6, 8, 14–16

U
Ukraine, 5, 10, 22
United States, 4–5, 16, 21, 26
uranium, 8–13, 15, 17–18, 20, 26

Y
yellowcake, 12